GRIEG
SELECTED WORKS FOR THE PIANO

EDITED BY HENRY LEVINE

About The Composer

1843, June 15. Edvard Grieg was born in Bergen, Norway, the son of the British Consul in Bergen. His mother's name was Gesine Judith Hagerup. Though his baptismal name included Hagerup, Grieg did not sanction its use as his middle name and never used it in his correspondence. When he was six years old he received his first musical instruction from his mother, a fine singer and accomplished pianist. At times Grieg rebelled at practicing, but his mother insisted on perfect performances (a familiar mother-child syndrome). On his own, young Grieg discovered with enchantment the world of harmony. In later years he wrote, "The world of harmony was always my dream-world." The music of Chopin and Schumann had a special appeal for him. He began to compose at the age of nine, but his first serious attempts were made between twelve and thirteen. At first he wanted to become a pastor, a prophet, or a herald. But at the age of fifteen his musical gifts were discovered by the famous Norwegian violinist, Ole Bull, a frequent visitor at the Grieg home. Ole Bull advised that Edvard be sent to Leipzig (Leipsic, then) to study at the Conservatorium to become a musician.

EDVARD GRIEG
(1843-1907)

1858–1862. At the Leipzig Conservatorium, Grieg studied piano with Plaidy, Wenzel and Moscheles; harmony and counterpoint with Richter, Papperitz and Hauptmann; score-reading with Reinecke. A contemporary student and companion was Arthur Sullivan, of later Gilbert and Sullivan fame.

1862. Passed his examination at the Conservatorium with credit, playing his own piano pieces, later published as Opus 1.

1863. Settled in Copenhagen, where he met Niels W. Gade, head of the Scandinavian School. At Gade's urging, Grieg wrote a symphony which was never published. Over the manuscript score Grieg wrote "Must never be performed." However, the second and third movements are now available in print as Opus 14, "Two Symphonic Pieces" for piano four hands.

1864. Renewed relation with Ole Bull, the champion of "Norse" music. They played sonatas and other duos together and made excursions into their favorite Norwegian mountain regions.

Second Edition
Copyright © MMVI by Alfred Publishing Co., Inc.
All rights reserved. Printed in USA.
ISBN 0-7390-1554-0

Cover art: Golden Autumn, 1895
by Isaac Levitan (1860–1900)
Tretyakov Gallery, Moscow, Russia
Scala/Art Resource, New York

Alfred has made every effort to make this book not only attractive but more useful and long-lasting as well. Usually, large books do not lie flat or stay open on the music rack. In addition, the pages (which are glued together) tend to break away from the spine after repeated use.

In this edition, pages are sewn together in multiples of 16. This special process prevents pages from falling out of the book while allowing it to stay open for ease in playing. We hope this unique binding will give you added pleasure and additional use.

1864. At Copenhagen, Grieg met Rikard Nordraak, a young and gifted Norwegian composer. Together they formed the Euterpe Society, to encourage young Northern composers and to espouse the cause of Norwegian music, freed from the Germanic shackles of Leipzig, without becoming faithless to the teachings of their mistress.

1864. Grieg became engaged to his cousin, Miss Nina Hagerup, a gifted singer, for whom he wrote the song "Jeg elsker dig" ("I Love Thee") to heartfelt words by Hans Christian Andersen. Her mother objected strenuously to Edvard as a prospective son-in-law. (He had this frustration in common with Robert Schumann, whose courtship of Clara Wieck had been vigorously opposed by her father. However, in both cases, love prevailed over parental oppositions.)

1865. First sojourn in Rome. Grieg wrote the overture, "In Autumn," his first orchestral work.

1866. Gave concert in Christiania (Oslo, now), the capital of Norway, with his fiancée. The program, probably the first one ever made up entirely of Norwegian music, was an encouraging success with the public and the press.

1866. The Philharmonic Society appointed Grieg its conductor, a post he held until 1874.

1867, June 11. Grieg married Nina Hagerup. Gave subscription concerts with his young wife, beside his Philharmonic commitments.

1868. At the age of twenty-five, Grieg composed his piano Concerto in A minor, Op. 16, during his summer vacation in the Danish village of Sölleröd.

1869. Edvard and Nina lost their daughter, aged thirteen months, the only child they ever had.

1869, April 3. Grieg played the solo part in the world première of his piano concerto in Copenhagen. It established his fame.

1870. Grieg's second sojourn in Rome. He showed his piano concerto to Liszt who played it perfectly at sight and concluded with these encouraging words to Grieg: "Keep steadily on; I tell you, you have the capability, and—do not let them intimidate you!"

1871. Founded the "Musical Society" with Johan Svendsen for performing choral works. Continued as conductor of the Philharmonic Society.

1874. Grieg was honored by the Norwegian government with an annuity of 1600 crowns for life. It enabled him to give up conducting and teaching, and to devote himself to composing and to giving concerts of his works at home and abroad.

1874. Grieg accepted an invitation from Henrik Ibsen, the Norwegian playwright, to compose incidental music to his play, "Peer Gynt." The music was originally published in the form of a piano duet. Subsequently, Grieg grouped his music into two orchestral suites, which made him known the world over as an original and fascinating composer.

1876, February 24. First performance of "Peer Gynt," with music, at the National Theatre in Christiania.

1885. Grieg built his elegant villa at Trollhaugen. (Troll means sprite; haug means hill.) It was beautifully situated on an inner branch of a fjord, about a half-hour's train ride from Bergen. He lived there for the rest of his life.

1907, July. Percy Grainger, the Australian pianist, with whom Grieg had established a warm friendship in England, was a guest at Trollhaugen for three weeks. Of Grainger, Grieg said, "He plays my Norwegian peasant dances as none of my countrymen can play them." Grainger later edited Grieg's piano concerto, with changes and suggestions which the composer had approved.

1907, September 4. Grieg died in Bergen at the age of sixty-four and was cremated. He received an imposing state funeral, mourned by many thousands of his countrymen. The urn containing his ashes was deposited in a grotto, selected by himself, visible from Trollhaugen.

Facsimile of Manuscript from "Peer Gynt" Suite by Edvard Grieg with facsimile of his autograph.

Honors

In recognition of his creative genius in music, Grieg received many honors from centers of learning and from music associations: appointed a member of the Swedish Academy of Music (1872); member of the Musical Academy at Leyden, Holland (1883); member of the French Academy of Fine Arts (1890); honorary degree of Doctor of Music conferred on him by the University of Cambridge, England (1893); honorary degree of Doctor of Music bestowed by Oxford University, England (1906). Grieg's sixtieth birthday, on June 15, 1903, was celebrated not only in the cities of Scandinavia but throughout Europe and America, many concerts of his music being devoted to a commemoration of the event. Grieg was particularly pleased when, in honor of this occasion, his bust was placed in the Gewandhaus concert hall in Leipzig, the city of his early music studies. Royalty, too, bestowed favors on the Griegs. They played and sang for Queen Victoria at Windsor, and were the guests of the German Kaiser Wilhelm on his yacht. But the adulation of the people was closer to his heart.

Grieg was held in high esteem by his contemporaries. Liszt was one of the first to recognize his distinctive qualities as a composer. Tchaikovsky, in the "Diary of My Tour in 1888," expressed his admiration for Grieg as a person and as a musician. He was impressed with the charm and poetic emotion of his music and confessed that he was powerfully attracted to "the gifted Norwegian." Tchaikovsky was touched to tears by Mme. Grieg's sympathetic singing of her husband's songs. MacDowell worshipped Grieg, to whom he dedicated two of his sonatas. In return, Grieg was high in his praise of MacDowell, whom he considered the most ideal of American composers. Brahms and Grieg mutually admired each other's works. Among the great pianists Paderewski, von Bülow, Pugno, Carreno and many others were ardent champions of Grieg's piano works.

Concert Tours

Grieg was in great demand as a composer, conductor and pianist. He appeared in these three capacities, with Mme. Grieg at times as assisting artist in the singing of his songs, in the principal music centers of Europe: Bergen, Oslo, Stockholm, Copenhagen, London, Birmingham, Berlin, Munich, Leipzig, Vienna, Prague, Warsaw, Amsterdam, Rome. In Paris occurred one of the most exciting episodes in Grieg's life. In 1899, Edouard Colonne invited Grieg to participate in a concert in Paris. Grieg, indignant over the Dreyfus affair, refused. In 1903, M. Colonne renewed the invitation with an explanatory and conciliatory letter. This time Grieg accepted. He was tumultuously greeted with cheers and hisses, reflecting the clash of musical and political sympathies. Grieg turned down tempting offers to appear in the United States, because he dreaded the sea voyage and the seasickness to which he was susceptible. He stipulated that he would come only if he got a written guarantee that "the Atlantic would behave itself."

The Piano Music of Grieg

Edvard Grieg was the dominant figure in the history of Norwegian music. In the folk tunes of his motherland he found musical inspiration and saw in them the nucleus of a Norwegian style of music. Only in rare cases, as in "Solvejg's Song," did he borrow the tunes outright. In his words, "My object in arranging this music for the pianoforte was to attempt to raise these folk tunes to an artistic level by harmonizing them in a style suitable for their nature. In my treatment of them I have tried to express my sense of the hidden harmonies of our folk airs." In his harmonic treatment he divined the appropriate chords and showed preference for chromatic progressions and modulations which he felt heightened the emotional content of the music. Grieg was fascinated, too, by the gay and spirited native dances, such as the halling (in 2/4 time) and the sprigdans (in 3/4 time), and used them with captivating effect. As a nationalist composer Grieg was to Norway what Chopin was to Poland, Tchaikovsky to Russia, Liszt to Hungary, and Dvořák to Bohemia, all of whom were influenced by their native folk music.

Because Grieg favored the smaller forms, he was referred to condescendingly as a "miniature" artist. His critics bewailed the fact that he "stuck in the fjord and never got out of it." Grieg resented this allusion and countered that his fame was based on his larger works, such as the piano concerto, the piano sonata, the violin and piano sonatas, and the Ballade. But size need not be a criterion of excellence. Grieg owes his popularity with piano students to his smaller pieces. They are musical gems, treated with simple charm and with a formal logic of their own not belabored with elaborate development.

In his piano music Grieg revealed such poetic fancy and beauty that Hans von Bülow called him "the Chopin of the North." Representative piano pieces are in the ten books of sixty-six Lyrical Pieces (Opus Nos. 12, 38, 43, 47, 54, 57, 62, 65, 68 and 71). The choice ones are in this collection. They reflect an exotic charm with strong nationalistic overtones. Since Grieg was an excellent pianist, they are pianistic as well as musically expressive. Deservedly they have been favorites over the years with piano students, teachers and the listening public. They should be played with a sensitive touch and with interpretative insight, and in the dance-inspired pieces with appropriate verve.

Grieg wrote 146 songs, many of which are small masterpieces. They reveal Grieg's poetic and musical sensibilities. Two of the songs, "Solvejg's Song" and "I Love Thee," are included in this collection in their effective arrangement for piano by the composer.

Editing: fingering, phrasing, pedaling, and dynamics that underscore the musical structure, have been added by Henry Levine.

Recommended biography, approved by Grieg: *Grieg and His Music,* by Henry T. Finck.

Titles: In most cases they are given in three languages—headed by English, with sub-titles in German, at left, and in Norwegian, at right. A single heading is used when the title is generic.

Grateful acknowledgment is extended to the Norwegian Information Service for linguistic help in the wording of the Norwegian titles to the piano pieces.

ALPHABETICAL INDEX

Page		Page	
22	Album-Leaf, Op. 12, No. 7	77	Morning-Mood, Op. 46, No. 1
30	Album-Leaf, Op. 28, No. 1	25	Norwegian Bridal Procession, Op. 19, No. 2
84	Anitra's Dance, Op. 46, No. 3	38	Norwegian Dance, Op. 35, No. 2
9	Arietta, Op. 12, No. 1	20	Norwegian Melody, Op. 12, No. 6
82	Ase's Death, Op. 46, No. 2	104	Notturno, Op. 54, No. 4
124	At Thy Feet, Op. 68, No. 3	24	Patriotic Song, Op 12, No. 8
42	Berceuse, Op. 38, No. 1	77	Peer Gynt Suite (First) Op, 46
64	Birdling, Op. 43, No. 4	77	1. Morning-Mood
58	Butterfly, Op. 43, No. 1	82	2. Ase's Death
128	By the Cradle, Op. 68, No. 5	84	3. Anitra's Dance
54	Canon, Op. 38, No. 8	88	4. In the Hall of the Mountain-King
34	Dance Caprice, Op. 28, No. 3	130	Puck, Op. 71, No. 3
50	Elegie, Op. 38, No. 6	134	Remembrances, Op. 71, No. 7
15	Elfin Dance, Op. 12, No. 4	118	Sailor's Song, Op. 68, No. 1
18	Folk-Song, Op. 12, No. 5	48	Skip-Dance, Op. 38, No. 5
46	Folk-Song, Op. 38, No. 2	62	Solitary Wanderer, Op. 43, No. 2
120	Grandmother's Minuet, Op. 68, No. 2	137	Solvejg's Song, Op. 52, No. 4
6	Humoreske, Op. 6, No. 2	93	Spring-Dance, Op. 47, No. 6
141	I Love Thee	70	To Spring, Op. 43, No. 6
88	In the Hall of the Mountain-King, Op. 46, No. 4	10	Waltz, Op. 12, No. 2
		52	Waltz, Op. 38, No. 7
66	Love-Poem, Op. 43, No. 5	13	Watchman's Song, Op. 12, No. 3
96	March of the Dwarfs, Op. 54, No. 3	108	Wedding-Day in Troldhaugen, Op. 65, No. 6

Humoreske

Op. 6, No. 2

Tempo di minuetto ed energico

Arietta

Op. 12, No. 1

Poco andante e sostenuto

* Note thematic resemblance with Remembrances, p. 134

Waltz

Walzer * Vals

Op. 12, No. 2

Allegro moderato

*In original edition, hands are reversed.

Watchman's Song
Wächterlied * Vaegtersang

Op. 12, No. 3

Molto andante e semplice

Elfin Dance
Elfentanz * Alfedans

Op. 12, No. 4

Folk-Song

Volksweise * Folkevise

Op. 12, No. 5

Norwegian Melody
Norwegisch * Norsk

Op. 12, No. 6

Presto marcato

Album-Leaf

Albumblatt ∗ Albumblad

Op. 12, No. 7

Patriotic Song

Vaterländisches Lied * Faedrelandssang

Maestoso   Op. 12, No. 8

Norwegian Bridal Procession

Norwegischer Brautzug im Vorüberziehen   *   Brudefölget drar forbi

Op. 19, No. 2

Album-Leaf
Albumblatt * Albumblad

Op. 28, No 1

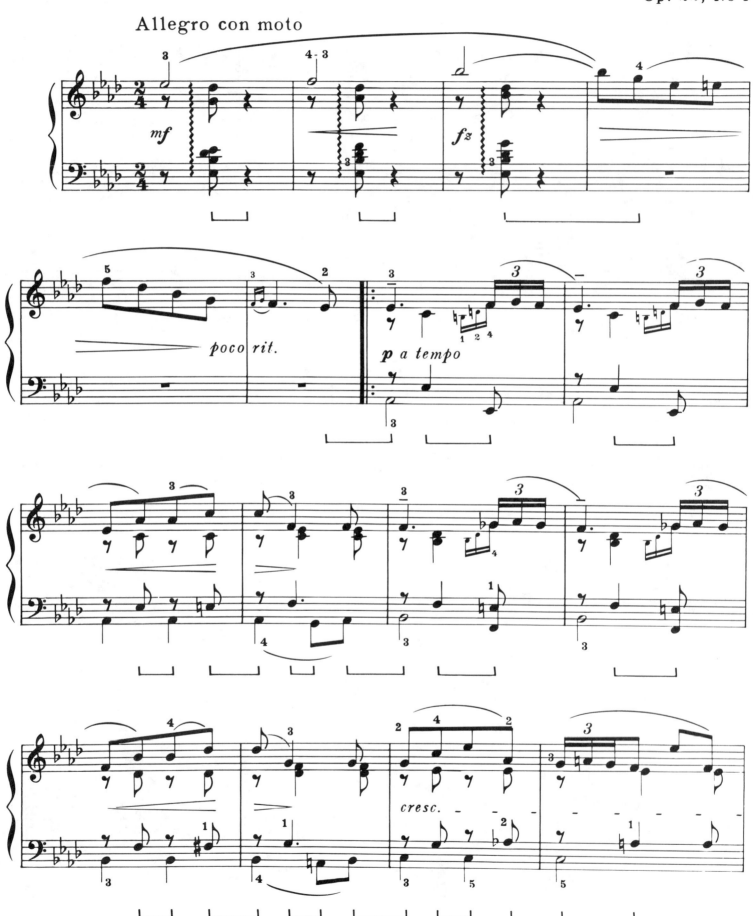

Dance Caprice

Op. 28, No. 3

Norwegian Dance

Norwegischer Tanz * Norsk Dans

Originally for piano duet

Op. 35, No. 2

Berceuse

Wiegenlied * Vuggevise

Op. 38, No. 1

Folk-Song

Volksweise ✱ Folkevise

Op. 38, No. 2

Skip-Dance
Springtanz * Springdans

Op. 38, No. 5

Elegie

Op. 38, No. 6

Waltz
Walzer * Vals

Op. 38, No. 7

Poco allegro

Canon

Kanon * Kanon

Op. 38, No. 8

Allegretto con moto

Minore Da Capo al Fine

Butterfly

Schmetterling * Summerfugl

Op. 43, No. 1

Allegro grazioso

Solitary Wanderer

Einsamer Wanderer ✶ Ensom Vandrer

Op. 43, No. 2

Allegretto semplice

*Hemiola

* Hemiola

Birdling

Vöglein ✴ Liten Fugl

Op. 43, No. 4

Allegro leggiero

Love-Poem
Erotik * Erotikk

Op. 43, No. 5

To Spring

An den Frühling * Til Foråret

Op. 43, No. 6

Allegro appassionato

Morning-Mood

Morgenstimmung   ∗   Morgenstemning

Composed as incidental orchestral music for Ibsen's play, *Peer Gynt*. Ibsen had written to Grieg: "... It is my intention to arrange *Peer Gynt* for performance on the stage. Will you compose the music which will be required?" Grieg agreed to. The first performance was on Feb. 24, 1876. Later Grieg developed the music into two orchestral suites (Op. 46 & Op. 52). Then it was arranged by the composer for piano duet and also for piano solo. The First Suite is the most famous. Its four numbers are: Morning-Mood, Ase's Death, Anitra's Dance, In the Hall of the Mountain-King.

In the play, Peer Gynt is depicted as a wild, lusty youth roaming in search of adventure and becoming involved in love affairs. His travels take him to the surrounding   s, to the coast of Morocco, through storms at sea, to the Sahara Desert, Egypt, Arabia, etc. The four numbers in this suite portray musically some episodes in his travels.

78

Ase's Death

Ases Tod * Aases Död

Peer Gynt returns home from his wanderings to be at the deathbed of his mother, Ase.

Op. 46, No. 2

Anitra's Dance

Anitras Tanz * Anitras Dans

Peer Gynt visits an Arab chieftain in his tent on an oasis. Peer is in Eastern dress and resting on cushions. Anitra and a troupe of girls dance and sing for him.

Op. 46, No. 3

Tempo di Mazurka

In the Hall of the Mountain-King

In der Halle des Bergkönigs * I Dovregubbens Hall

Peer Gynt at a wedding ceremony, abducts Ingrid, the bride of one of the villagers, and to their consternation, vanishes with her in an invisible cloak. They land on a mountain-side. Peer Gynt quickly tires of her and curtly sends her back home. As he wanders about, he finds the royal hall of the legendary Mountain-King, whose daughter falls in love with him. Peer spurns her. The enraged mountain-folk, hobglobins, trolls, gnomes and elves show their displeasure in ghoulish dances depicted in this music.

Spring-Dance

Springtanz ✱ Springdans

Op. 47, No. 6

March of the Dwarfs

Zug der Zwerge * Trolltog

Op. 54, No. 3

Notturno

Op. 54, No. 4

Wedding-Day in Troldhaugen

Hochzeitstag auf Troldhaugen * Bryllupsdag på Trollhaugen

Op. 65, No. 6

Tempo di Marcia un poco vivace

*Grieg's country home.

Sailor's Song

Matrosenlied * Matrosernes Opsang

Allegro vivace e marcato

Op. 68, No. 1

Grandmother's Minuet

Grossmutters Menuett * Bedstemors Menuett

Op. 68, No. 2

Allegretto grazioso e leggierissimo

At Thy Feet

Zu deinen Füssen * For dine Födder

Op. 68, No. 3

Poco andante e molto espressivo

By the Cradle

An der Wiege * Bådnlåt

Allegretto tranquillamente

Op. 68, No. 5

Puck

Kobold * Småtrold

Op. 71, No. 3

Remembrances

Nachklänge * Efterklang

Op. 71, No. 7

*Reminiscent of theme of Arietta, Op. 12, No. 1; page 9.

Solvejg's Song

Solvejgs Lied * Solveigs sang

God help thee, whil-ev-er His sun thou dost feel, His sun thou dost feel,

God bless thee, when-e'er at His feet thou dost kneel, at His feet thou dost kneel.

Here I shall a-wait thee till thou art near, till thou art near, And

if thou stay up yon-der, then I shall meet thee there, then I shall meet thee